GROWING KALE

FOR BUSINESS

Complete Beginners Guide To Understand And Master How To Grow Kale From Scratch (Cultivation, Care, Management, Harvest, Profit And More)

HARRISON DAMON

DISCLAIMER

The information provided in this book, is intended for informational purposes only. The author makes no representations or warranties of any kind, express or implied, about the completeness, accuracy, reliability, suitability, or availability of the information contained in this book. Any reliance you place on such information is strictly at your own risk.

The author shall not be liable for any loss or damage arising from the use of this book or the information contained herein. It is your responsibility to conduct thorough research and seek professional advice before making any decisions based on the content of this book.

This book may contain references or mentions of individuals, products, websites, organizations, or other names for illustrative purposes only. The author does not endorse, recommend, or have any affiliation with the mentioned entities unless explicitly stated

Table of Contents

CHAPTER ONE

INTRODUCTION TO KALE FARMING
The Rise of Kale as a Superfood

Introduction

Kale, once a humble leafy green relegated to the sidelines of salad bowls, has experienced a meteoric rise in popularity over the past decade. Its transformation from a garnish to a superfood has captivated health-conscious consumers and culinary enthusiasts alike. This surge in demand has positioned kale as a lucrative crop for farmers looking to capitalize on the growing health and wellness trend.

Nutritional Prowess

Kale's ascent to superfood status is primarily attributed to its exceptional nutritional profile. Packed with vitamins A, C, and K, along with essential minerals like calcium and iron, kale stands out as a nutrient powerhouse. Additionally, it is rich in antioxidants and fiber, making it a preferred choice for those seeking a diet that promotes overall well-being.

Culinary Versatility

Beyond its nutritional benefits, kale has gained popularity due to its versatility in the kitchen. From salads to smoothies, soups, and even kale chips, this leafy green has found its way into a myriad of dishes. Its robust flavor and hearty texture make it an appealing addition to both traditional and contemporary recipes, further contributing to its widespread consumption.

Celebrity Endorsement

The rise of kale has been fueled by celebrity endorsements and the influence of wellness advocates. High-profile chefs, nutritionists, and fitness experts have championed kale as a must-have ingredient in a balanced diet. This celebrity backing has not only propelled kale into the mainstream but has also created a cultural phenomenon around the green superfood.

Health and Sustainability

In an era where consumers are increasingly conscious of their health and the environmental impact of their food choices, kale shines as a sustainable and health-promoting option. Its ability to thrive in various climates and resist pests naturally makes it an attractive choice for environmentally conscious farmers and consumers alike.

Market Trends and Opportunities

Increasing Demand

The kale market is experiencing an upward trajectory, with demand steadily rising across the globe. Consumers are actively seeking nutrient-dense foods, and kale, with its impressive health benefits, has become a sought-after commodity in the fresh produce sector. As dietary preferences shift towards plant-based options, the demand for kale is expected to continue its upward trend.

Growing Popularity in Foodservice

One notable market trend is the increasing adoption of kale by the food service industry. Restaurants, cafes, and catering services are incorporating kale into their menus, catering to the growing demand for healthier and more diverse food options. This presents a significant opportunity for kale farmers to establish partnerships with food service providers and tap into this expanding market.

Export Opportunities

The international market for kale is expanding, creating opportunities for farmers to explore export avenues. Countries with a rising health-conscious consumer base are importing kale to meet the demand for this superfood. Understanding the regulatory requirements and establishing efficient supply chains can position kale farmers to take advantage of global market trends.

Diversification of Kale Varieties

The kale market is evolving with the introduction of diverse kale varieties. Beyond the traditional curly kale, new cultivars, such as Lacinato (or dinosaur kale) and Red Russian kale, are gaining popularity. Diversifying the types of kale grown can allow farmers to cater to specific consumer preferences and tap into niche markets.

Benefits of Growing Kale for Business

High-Profit Potential

Growing kale for business offers a compelling financial incentive. With the increasing demand and market trends favoring this superfood, farmers stand to benefit from a high profit potential. The relatively low production costs, coupled with the ability to sell kale at premium prices, make it an attractive venture for entrepreneurs in the agricultural sector.

Short Growth Cycle

One of the advantages of kale farming is its short growth cycle. Unlike some crops that require an extended period before harvest, kale matures relatively quickly. This allows for multiple planting and harvesting cycles within a single growing season, enabling farmers to generate a consistent income throughout the year.

Crop Resilience

Kale is renowned for its resilience to various environmental conditions and pests. Its hardiness makes it a reliable crop that can withstand fluctuations in weather and resist common pests without the need for excessive chemical interventions. This resilience contributes to a more stable and sustainable farming enterprise.

Health and Environmental Impact

Cultivating kale aligns with the increasing emphasis on health and environmental sustainability. As a nutrient-dense and eco-friendly crop, kale farming enables businesses to contribute to healthier diets and environmentally conscious agriculture practices. This dual benefit resonates with consumers and enhances the overall appeal of kale as a business venture.

Diversification and Risk Mitigation

For farmers seeking to diversify their crops and mitigate risks associated with relying on a single commodity, kale offers an excellent option. Its rising demand and adaptability provide a valuable addition to a diversified agricultural portfolio. This can help farmers safeguard their income against market fluctuations and unforeseen challenges in the agricultural sector.

CHAPTER TWO

UNDERSTANDING KALE VARIETIES
Exploring Different Kale Varieties

Kale, a versatile and nutrient-rich leafy green, comes in various varieties, each with its unique characteristics and flavors. As a prospective business owner venturing into kale cultivation, it's crucial to delve into the diverse world of kale varieties to make informed decisions and cater to a broader market.

Curly Kale Varieties

Curly kale varieties, such as Winterbor and Redbor, are known for their tightly curled leaves, adding texture and visual appeal to dishes. These varieties are hardy and can withstand colder temperatures, making them ideal choices for businesses operating in regions with diverse climates. Their robust flavor profile makes them popular in salads, smoothies, and as an attractive garnish.

Lacinato Kale Varieties

Lacinato kale, also known as Dinosaur kale, boasts long, narrow, dark green leaves. This variety is recognized for its deep, earthy flavor and tender texture. Lacinato kale is often preferred in cooked dishes, such as soups, stews, and sautés. Its unique appearance and rich taste make it a favorite among health-conscious consumers, providing a distinct market niche for businesses focusing on premium kale products.

Red Russian Kale Varieties

With its striking purple stems and fringed leaves, Red Russian kale is not only visually appealing but also offers a mild and sweet flavor. This variety is popular in both raw and cooked preparations, making it a versatile option for businesses aiming to cater to a wide range of culinary preferences. The vibrant color of Red Russian kale adds an aesthetic touch to salads and can elevate the visual appeal of packaged kale products.

Siberian Kale Varieties

Siberian kale, characterized by its blue-green, finely curled leaves, is known for its cold resistance and ability to thrive in various growing conditions. This robust kale variety is an excellent choice for businesses looking to ensure a consistent and reliable harvest throughout the year. Siberian kale's hearty nature makes it suitable for a variety of culinary applications, including stir-fries, smoothies, and juicing.

Selecting the Right Kale for Your Business

Choosing the right kale variety for your business involves a careful consideration of factors such as climate, market demand, and culinary trends. The decision-making process is integral to the success of your kale cultivation venture, influencing not only the quality of your produce but also your business's overall profitability.

Climate Considerations

Understanding your local climate is paramount when selecting a kale variety for cultivation. If your region experiences harsh winters, opting for cold-resistant varieties like Winterbor or Siberian kale ensures a year-round supply. Conversely, in milder climates, the choice may lean towards more delicate varieties like

Red Russian or Lacinato kale. Tailoring your kale selection to your specific climate mitigates risks and maximizes yield potential.

Market Demand and Trends

Analyzing market trends and consumer preferences is a key aspect of selecting the right kale variety. Conduct market research to identify popular kale varieties in your target demographic. For instance, if there is a growing demand for gourmet salads, emphasizing curly kale varieties might be strategic. Staying attuned to health and wellness trends can also guide your selection, as certain varieties like Lacinato kale are often associated with premium, nutrient-rich offerings.

Culinary Versatility

Consider the culinary versatility of each kale variety to diversify your product offerings. If your business plans include supplying restaurants or catering services, having a mix of kale varieties suitable for both raw and cooked applications can broaden your customer base. Offering a range of options allows you to tap into various culinary preferences and ensures that your kale products are sought after by a wider audience.

Factors Influencing Kale Variety Choice

Several factors influence the choice of kale varieties for commercial cultivation. From agronomic considerations to consumer preferences, understanding these factors is essential for making informed decisions that contribute to the success and sustainability of your kale business.

Agronomic Considerations

Each kale variety has specific agronomic requirements, including soil type, water needs, and sunlight tolerance. Understanding these factors is crucial for optimizing cultivation practices and ensuring a healthy, productive crop. Conducting soil tests and consulting with agricultural experts can help you tailor your cultivation methods to the specific needs of your chosen kale varieties, ultimately enhancing crop yields and quality.

Pest and Disease Resistance

Different kale varieties exhibit varying levels of resistance to pests and diseases. Assessing the prevalence of specific pests in your region and selecting kale varieties with natural resistance can significantly reduce the need for pesticides and other interventions. This not only aligns with sustainable farming practices but also contributes to the production of healthier, more marketable kale. Harvesting and Storage Considerations Understanding the harvesting and storage characteristics of each kale variety is essential for efficient farm management and post-harvest handling. Some varieties may have longer shelf lives or be more amenable to mechanical harvesting, streamlining your operational processes. Aligning your choice of kale varieties with your preferred harvesting and storage methods can enhance overall efficiency and reduce waste.

In conclusion, exploring the diverse kale varieties, selecting the right ones for your business, and considering various influencing factors are crucial steps in the successful cultivation of kale for commercial purposes. By embracing the unique qualities of each kale variety and aligning them with market demand and agronomic considerations, you can position your business for sustained growth and profitability in the dynamic kale market.

CHAPTER THREE

PLANNING YOUR KALE FARM
Site Selection and Soil Preparation
for Your Kale Farm

When planning your kale farm for business, one of the crucial initial steps is selecting the right site and preparing the soil for optimal kale cultivation. The success of your venture heavily relies on a judicious choice of location and soil quality.

Site Selection

Choosing an appropriate site involves considering various factors. First and foremost, assess the sunlight exposure the location receives throughout the day. Kale thrives in full sunlight, so select a site with at least six to eight hours of direct sunlight. Additionally, ensure that the chosen site has proper drainage to prevent waterlogging, which could be detrimental to kale plants.

Proximity to water sources is another key aspect. While kale is known for its resilience in various conditions, having easy access to water facilitates irrigation, especially during dry spells. Additionally, consider the wind patterns in the area, as strong winds can damage kale plants. Planting in a location with some windbreaks, such as natural barriers or structures, can protect your crop.

Soil Preparation

Once you've selected the ideal site, focus on soil preparation. Kale thrives in well-draining soil with a slightly acidic to neutral pH level (around 6.0 to 7.0). Conduct a soil test to determine the current pH and nutrient levels. If necessary, amend the soil with organic matter, such as compost or well-rotted manure, to enhance its fertility.

Clear the selected area of any debris, rocks, or weeds that might interfere with kale growth. Utilize cover crops during the off-season to prevent soil erosion and improve soil structure. Implementing a crop rotation plan can also help control pests and diseases, ensuring a healthier kale crop.

In summary, meticulous site selection and soil preparation lay the foundation for a successful kale farm. Attention to sunlight, water access, wind patterns, and soil quality is pivotal for ensuring a conducive environment for kale cultivation.

Climate Considerations for Your Kale Farm Business

Understanding the climate is fundamental for planning and managing a successful kale farm business. Kale is a versatile crop that can adapt to various climates, but specific considerations are essential to optimize growth and yield.

Temperature Requirements

Kale is a cool-season crop that thrives in moderate temperatures. The ideal temperature range for kale cultivation is between 55°F to 75°F (13°C to 24°C). While kale can withstand light frosts, prolonged exposure to extreme cold can lead to reduced quality and yield. Therefore, it's crucial to choose the right kale varieties that align with your local climate.

Seasonal Planning

To maximize kale production, plan your planting schedule according to the local seasons. In cooler climates, kale can be grown year-round with successive plantings. In warmer regions, focus on cultivating kale during the cooler months to avoid heat stress on the plants. Understanding your local climate patterns and adjusting your planting calendar accordingly is essential for a consistent and successful kale harvest.

Water Management

Proper irrigation is critical, especially during periods of low rainfall or drought. Kale requires consistent moisture to thrive, and a well-thought-out irrigation system should be in place. Mulching can also help retain soil moisture and regulate temperature, creating a more stable environment for kale plants.

In conclusion, a comprehensive understanding of your local climate is indispensable for a thriving kale farm business. Tailor your cultivation practices to the temperature ranges, seasons, and water availability in your region to ensure optimal kale growth and productivity.

Designing an Efficient Kale Farm Layout for Business Success

The layout of your kale farm plays a pivotal role in optimizing efficiency, productivity, and overall business success. A well-designed layout not only enhances the visual appeal but also streamlines operations and facilitates better management.

Row Arrangement and Spacing

Consider the layout of your kale rows carefully. Adequate spacing between rows is essential for easy access, efficient harvesting, and pest control. Typically, spacing kale rows 18 to 24 inches apart allows for optimal air circulation and sunlight exposure, reducing the risk of diseases. Additionally, plan for wider aisles to accommodate machinery and facilitate smooth navigation during various farming activities.

Crop Rotation and Companion Planting

Incorporate a crop rotation strategy to prevent soil-borne diseases and maintain soil fertility. Avoid planting kale in the same location season after season. Instead, rotate with other crops to break disease cycles and optimize nutrient utilization. Consider companion planting with compatible crops to enhance pest control and promote overall ecosystem health.

Infrastructure and Facilities

Invest in essential infrastructure and facilities for your kale farm. This includes irrigation systems, storage facilities, and shade structures if needed. Efficient irrigation systems ensure consistent moisture, while adequate storage helps manage harvested produce effectively. Shade structures can protect young plants from excessive sunlight during peak hours.

Accessibility and Ergonomics

Design your kale farm layout with accessibility and ergonomics in mind. This includes positioning storage areas, workstations, and equipment sheds strategically. Minimize the distance workers need to cover for various tasks, reducing fatigue and improving overall efficiency. Additionally, ergonomic considerations enhance worker comfort and safety. In conclusion, a well-thought-out kale farm layout is a cornerstone for business success. Prioritize row spacing, crop rotation, infrastructure, and ergonomic considerations to create an efficient and productive environment for your kale cultivation venture.

CHAPTER FOUR

PLANNING AND ESTABLISHING YOUR PEA FARM

Identifying Necessary Farming Equipment

Successful kale farming begins with the right tools and equipment. Identifying and investing in the necessary farming equipment is crucial for ensuring a smooth and efficient operation. Here are the key components you need to consider:

1. Tillage Equipment: To prepare the soil for kale cultivation, you'll need appropriate tillage equipment. Tractors equipped with plows, disc harrows, and cultivators are essential for breaking up the soil, removing weeds, and creating a suitable seedbed. Proper soil preparation is fundamental to the success of your kale farm.

2. Planting Tools: Precision in planting is essential for maximizing yield. Invest in seed drills or planters that provide accurate spacing between kale plants. This ensures uniform growth and facilitates easier weed management. Additionally, consider hand tools for smaller-scale operations or areas where machinery might not be practical.

3. Irrigation System: An adequate water supply is vital for kale cultivation. Depending on your location and farm size, choose an irrigation system that suits your needs. Drip irrigation is a sustainable choice, minimizing water wastage and promoting efficient water delivery directly to the plants' roots.

4. Harvesting Equipment: The timing and method of harvest impact the quality of your kale produce. Mechanical harvesters are available for larger-scale operations, but hand harvesters may be necessary for smaller plots or specialty varieties. Ensure your equipment is sharp and well-maintained to avoid damage to the plants during harvesting.

5. Storage and Processing Tools: After harvest, proper storage is crucial to maintain the freshness and nutritional value of kale. Invest in cooling and storage facilities like walk-in coolers or refrigerated trucks. If you plan to process kale into value-added products like pre-cut salads or frozen kale, consider the necessary processing equipment such as cutting machines and packaging tools.

Subheading: Sustainable Practices in Kale Farming

Sustainability in kale farming not only benefits the environment but also contributes to the long-term success of your business. Implementing eco-friendly practices can enhance soil health, reduce resource consumption, and create a positive brand image. Here are key sustainable practices to consider:

1. Crop Rotation: Rotate your kale crops with other vegetables or cover crops to prevent soil depletion and minimize the risk of pests and diseases. This practice enhances soil fertility and reduces the need for synthetic fertilizers.

2. Organic Fertilization: Choose organic fertilizers rich in nitrogen, phosphorus, and potassium to nourish your kale plants. Compost and well-rotted manure are excellent alternatives, promoting soil structure and microbial activity while avoiding the negative environmental impacts associated with chemical fertilizers.

3. Integrated Pest Management (IPM): Adopt an IPM approach to control pests and diseases. Utilize beneficial insects, natural predators, and resistant kale varieties to minimize the reliance on chemical pesticides. Regular monitoring of your crops will enable you to intervene promptly and effectively.

4. Water Conservation: Implement water-saving technologies such as rainwater harvesting and efficient irrigation systems. Collecting rainwater reduces dependence on external water sources, and drip irrigation minimizes water wastage by delivering water directly to the plant roots.

5. Cover Cropping: Plant cover crops during the off-season to protect and improve soil structure. Cover crops contribute organic matter, suppress weeds, and prevent soil erosion, promoting a sustainable and resilient farming system.

Subheading: Technology Integration for Efficiency

In the modern era, technology plays a pivotal role in enhancing efficiency and productivity in kale farming. Integrating the latest agricultural technologies can streamline operations and provide valuable insights.

Here's how you can leverage technology for optimal results:

1. Precision Farming: Utilize GPS technology and sensors to implement precision farming techniques. This includes precise planting, nutrient application, and irrigation, resulting in resource-efficient and high-yield kale production.

2. Farm Management Software: Invest in farm management software to monitor and manage various aspects of your kale farm, including inventory, crop rotation schedules, and financial records. This technology enables data-driven decision-making and enhances overall farm efficiency.

3. Drone Technology: Drones equipped with cameras and sensors can provide valuable data on crop health, allowing for early detection of diseases, nutrient deficiencies, or pest infestations. This proactive approach enables timely intervention and minimizes crop losses.

4. Automated Harvesting Systems: Explore the possibility of automated harvesting systems, especially for large-scale kale farms. Robotic harvesters equipped with computer vision technology can efficiently and accurately harvest kale, reducing labor costs and increasing overall productivity.

5. Climate Monitoring Sensors: Install climate monitoring sensors to track temperature, humidity, and other environmental factors. This data helps you optimize growing conditions, adjust irrigation schedules, and protect your kale crops from adverse weather conditions.

By meticulously planning and integrating these components into your kale farming venture, you'll set the foundation for a sustainable, efficient, and technologically advanced operation, ensuring long-term success in the kale market.

CHAPTER FIVE

Essential Equipment and Tools
Seed Selection and Quality

Choosing the right seeds is a critical step in successfully growing kale for business. The quality of your seeds directly influences the overall yield and health of your kale plants. When selecting seeds for commercial kale cultivation, it's essential to prioritize factors such as disease resistance, germination rate, and variety suitability for your specific growing conditions.

Varietal Considerations: Begin by researching and selecting kale varieties that are well-suited for your target market and growing region. Consider factors such as taste, texture, and appearance, as these aspects play a crucial role in consumer preferences. Supplier Reputation: Opt for reputable seed suppliers known for delivering high-quality seeds. Reading customer reviews, checking for certifications, and seeking recommendations from experienced growers can help ensure you source seeds from reliable providers.

Germination Testing: Before planting on a larger scale, conduct germination tests on a small batch of seeds. This process allows you to assess the viability of the seeds and estimate the germination rate. High germination rates contribute to uniform plant growth and a more predictable harvest.

Disease Resistance: Kale is susceptible to certain diseases, such as downy mildew and black rot. Choose seeds with built-in resistance to common kale diseases to minimize the risk of crop loss. Disease-resistant varieties not only enhance plant health but also reduce the need for chemical interventions.

Best Practices for Seeding

Proper seeding practices lay the foundation for a successful kale cultivation venture. Whether you're starting seeds indoors or directly sowing them in the field, adhering to best practices ensures optimal germination, uniform growth, and ultimately, a bountiful harvest.

Timing and Seasonality: Understanding the ideal timing for seeding is crucial. Kale is a cool-season crop, so plan your seeding schedule to coincide with the recommended planting window for your region. This will maximize the favorable growing conditions and lead to healthier plants.

Seed Depth and Spacing: Follow recommended guidelines for seed depth and spacing to prevent overcrowding and competition among plants. Proper spacing ensures adequate sunlight exposure, air circulation, and nutrient absorption, all essential for robust kale growth.

Germination Environment: Create a conducive environment for germination by maintaining consistent moisture levels, optimal temperature, and adequate lighting. Utilize seed trays, heat mats, and grow lights as needed to provide the ideal conditions for the early stages of kale development.

Thinning Practices: Once seedlings have emerged, thin them to ensure proper spacing and allow the strongest plants to thrive. Thinning helps prevent overcrowding, reduces the risk of disease transmission, and promotes vigorous growth by minimizing competition for resources.

Transplanting Seedlings for Optimal Growth

Transplanting seedlings marks a crucial phase in the kale cultivation process. This step requires careful attention to detail to ensure the successful establishment of plants in their final growing location. Follow these best practices for transplanting seedlings to promote optimal growth and maximize yield.

Hardening Off: Before transplanting, gradually acclimate seedlings to outdoor conditions through a process known as hardening off. This involves exposing the seedlings to outdoor elements such as sunlight, wind, and fluctuating temperatures over some time. Hardening off prepares the plants for the transition from a controlled indoor environment to an open field.

Soil Preparation: Prepare the transplant site by cultivating the soil and incorporating organic matter. Kale thrives in well-draining soil with a slightly acidic to neutral pH. Ensure that the soil is rich in nutrients, promoting healthy root development and overall plant vitality.

Planting Depth and Spacing: Transplant seedlings at the appropriate depth, ensuring that the roots are well-covered, and the soil is firmly packed around the base of the plant. Maintain recommended spacing between plants to allow for optimal air circulation, minimize disease risk, and maximize sunlight exposure.

Watering Practices: Water newly transplanted seedlings consistently to help them establish strong root systems. Gradually reduce watering frequency as the plants mature, but always monitor soil moisture levels to prevent drought stress, which can adversely affect kale growth and quality.

By adhering to these best practices, you can enhance the success of your kale cultivation business, from selecting top-quality seeds to facilitating robust seedling growth and seamless transplanting for optimal plant development.

CHAPTER SIX

NUTRIENT MANAGEMENT AND FERTILIZATION

Understanding Kale Nutrient Requirements

Kale, a nutrient-dense leafy green, thrives when provided with the right balance of essential nutrients. Understanding the specific nutrient requirements of kale is crucial for successful cultivation and a thriving business. Kale is known for its high demand for nitrogen, phosphorus, and potassium (NPK), as well as secondary and micronutrients. Nitrogen plays a vital role in promoting leafy growth, while phosphorus aids in root development and overall plant energy transfer. Potassium is essential for disease resistance and stress tolerance.

To determine the nutrient needs of your kale crop, soil testing is an invaluable tool. Soil analysis helps identify existing nutrient levels, enabling growers to make informed decisions about fertilization. The pH level of the soil also influences nutrient availability, and maintaining an optimal pH range for kale cultivation (around 6.0 to 7.5) ensures that nutrients are readily absorbed by the plants.

Additionally, understanding kale's growth stages is crucial for tailoring nutrient applications. During the early stages, nitrogen-rich fertilizers promote vigorous leaf development, while later stages benefit from balanced formulations to support overall plant health. Adjusting nutrient applications based on growth phases ensures efficient resource utilization and maximizes yield potential.

Organic and Synthetic Fertilizer Options

Choosing the right fertilizers is a pivotal decision in kale cultivation, especially when aiming for a business-oriented approach. Organic and synthetic fertilizers each have their merits, and growers must weigh the benefits and drawbacks of each.

Organic Fertilizers: Organic options include compost, manure, and other natural sources of nutrients. These fertilizers contribute to soil health by enhancing microbial activity and promoting sustainable farming practices. However, their nutrient release is often slower compared to synthetic counterparts, requiring thoughtful planning to meet kale's specific growth demands.

Synthetic Fertilizers: Synthetic fertilizers offer precise control over nutrient concentrations and are readily available to plants. They provide a quick and targeted solution to nutrient deficiencies, which can be crucial for commercial kale production. However, over-reliance on synthetic fertilizers may lead to imbalances, soil degradation, and environmental concerns.

Many growers opt for a hybrid approach, combining organic and synthetic fertilizers to harness the benefits of both. This approach promotes sustainability while addressing immediate nutrient needs. Regardless of the chosen fertilizer type, proper application rates and timing are essential to prevent nutrient excesses or deficiencies.

Implementing Effective Fertilization Strategies

To optimize kale production for business, implementing effective fertilization strategies is paramount.

Precision Fertilization: Tailoring nutrient applications to the specific needs of the crop and growth stages is essential. Employing precision fertilization techniques, such as split applications or foliar feeding, ensures that kale receives nutrients when they are most beneficial. This approach maximizes nutrient use efficiency and minimizes waste.

Seasonal Adjustments: Recognizing the seasonal variations in nutrient requirements is crucial for successful kale cultivation. Adjusting fertilizer formulations and application rates based on seasonal demands, such as increased nitrogen during rapid growth periods, prevents nutrient imbalances and fosters healthy plant development.

Soil Amendments: Incorporating soil amendments, such as organic matter, helps improve soil structure and nutrient retention. This practice enhances the overall fertility of the soil, reducing the reliance on external fertilizers over time. Composted materials and cover crops are valuable additions that contribute to a sustainable and resilient nutrient management system.

Monitoring and Adaptation: Regular monitoring of soil nutrient levels, plant health, and growth patterns is fundamental for adapting fertilization strategies as needed. This proactive approach allows growers to identify potential issues before they escalate, ensuring a consistent and high-quality kale yield.

In conclusion, successful kale cultivation for business requires a comprehensive understanding of nutrient requirements, thoughtful selection of fertilizers, and the implementation of effective fertilization strategies. By combining knowledge of kale's growth stages with precision fertilization techniques, growers can optimize nutrient utilization, promote sustainable practices, and ultimately yield a bountiful harvest for the market.

CHAPTER SEVEN

PEST AND DISEASE MANAGEMENT

Identifying Common Kale Pests and Diseases

Kale, a nutrient-rich leafy green, is susceptible to various pests and diseases that can compromise its growth and overall health. Identifying these issues early on is crucial for successful kale cultivation. Here are some common pests and diseases that kale growers should be aware of:

1. Aphids (Aphidoidea):

Aphids are small, sap-sucking insects that can quickly multiply and cause damage to kale plants. They often cluster on the undersides of leaves, causing them to curl and distort. Regular inspection of the leaves is essential for early detection.

2. Cabbage Worms (Pieris rapae):

Cabbage worms are the larvae of white butterflies and can devastate kale crops by feeding on the leaves. Look for small green caterpillars and their droppings.

Floating row covers can be used to protect plants from adult butterflies.

3. Downy Mildew (Peronospora parasitica):

Downy mildew is a common fungal disease that affects kale. It manifests as yellowish spots on the upper surface of leaves with a downy appearance on the undersides. Proper spacing between plants and good air circulation can help prevent the spread of this disease.

4. Clubroot (Plasmodiophora brassicae):

Clubroot is a soil-borne disease that affects the roots, causing swelling and deformities. It thrives in acidic soils. Maintaining proper soil pH and practicing crop rotation are effective preventive measures against clubroot.

5. Whiteflies (Aleyrodidae):

Whiteflies are tiny, winged insects that feed on the sap of kale plants, leading to reduced vigor and yellowing of leaves. Yellow sticky traps and introducing natural predators like ladybugs can help control whitefly populations.

Integrated Pest Management (IPM) Techniques

To effectively manage pests and diseases in kale cultivation, implementing Integrated Pest Management (IPM) techniques is crucial. IPM focuses on sustainable and environmentally friendly approaches to minimize the use of chemical pesticides. Here are key strategies for a successful IPM program:

1. Regular Monitoring and Scouting:

Conduct regular inspections of kale plants to identify pest and disease issues early. Monitor the undersides of leaves, stems, and the soil around the plants. Early detection allows for prompt intervention.

2. Biological Control:

Introduce natural predators and beneficial insects, such as ladybugs, lacewings, and parasitic wasps, to control pest populations. These organisms can help maintain a balance in the ecosystem without resorting to chemical interventions.

3. Cultural Practices:

Implement cultural practices like crop rotation, proper spacing, and companion planting to disrupt the life cycles of pests and diseases. These practices reduce the risk of buildup in the soil and limit the spread of pathogens.

4. Resistant Varieties:

Choose kale varieties that exhibit resistance to common pests and diseases. Resistant plants are less likely to succumb to infestations, providing a natural defense against potential threats.

5. Organic Sprays and Neem Oil:

Utilize organic sprays and neem oil as alternatives to synthetic pesticides. Neem oil, in particular, has insecticidal properties and can be an effective tool in managing certain pests while minimizing harm to beneficial insects.

Natural and Organic Solutions for Pest Control

Embracing natural and organic solutions is not only environmentally friendly but also promotes the production of healthier and more sustainable kale.

Here are some effective natural and organic methods for pest control in kale cultivation:

1. Neem Oil:

Neem oil, derived from the neem tree, acts as a natural pesticide. It disrupts the feeding and reproductive cycles of pests while being safe for beneficial insects. Regular application can help deter aphids, whiteflies, and other pests.

2. Garlic Spray:

Garlic has natural insect-repelling properties. Create a garlic spray by blending garlic cloves with water and applying it to kale plants. This can help deter pests without harming the environment.

3. Diatomaceous Earth:

Diatomaceous earth is a powdery substance that consists of fossilized diatoms. Sprinkle it around kale plants to create a barrier that dehydrates and kills insects upon contact. It's an effective method for controlling crawling pests.

4. Companion Planting:

Planting kale alongside companion plants that naturally repel pests can be beneficial. For example, planting aromatic herbs like basil and cilantro can help deter pests and enhance the overall health of the kale crop.

5. Beneficial Nematodes:

Beneficial nematodes are microscopic organisms that prey on soil-dwelling pests, including larvae of insects like cabbage worms. Applying nematodes to the soil can help control pest populations without resorting to chemical interventions.

In conclusion, successful kale cultivation for business involves proactive identification of pests and diseases, implementing integrated pest management techniques, and embracing natural and organic solutions. By combining these approaches, growers can foster a healthy and resilient kale crop while minimizing the environmental impact of pest control measures.

CHAPTER EIGHT

NUTRIENT MANAGEMENT AND FERTILIZATION

Understanding Kale Nutrient Requirements

Kale, a nutrient-dense leafy green, thrives when provided with the right balance of essential nutrients. Understanding the specific nutrient requirements of kale is crucial for successful cultivation and a thriving business. Kale is known for its high demand for nitrogen, phosphorus, and potassium (NPK), as well as secondary and micronutrients. Nitrogen plays a vital role in promoting leafy growth, while phosphorus aids in root development and overall plant energy transfer. Potassium is essential for disease resistance and stress tolerance.

To determine the nutrient needs of your kale crop, soil testing is an invaluable tool. Soil analysis helps identify existing nutrient levels, enabling growers to make informed decisions about fertilization. The pH level of the soil also influences nutrient availability, and maintaining an optimal pH range for kale cultivation (around 6.0 to 7.5) ensures that nutrients are readily absorbed by the plants.

Additionally, understanding kale's growth stages is crucial for tailoring nutrient applications. During the early stages, nitrogen-rich fertilizers promote vigorous leaf development, while later stages benefit from balanced formulations to support overall plant health. Adjusting nutrient applications based on growth phases ensures efficient resource utilization and maximizes yield potential.

Organic and Synthetic Fertilizer Options

Choosing the right fertilizers is a pivotal decision in kale cultivation, especially when aiming for a business-oriented approach. Organic and synthetic fertilizers each have their merits, and growers must weigh the benefits and drawbacks of each.

Organic Fertilizers: Organic options include compost, manure, and other natural sources of nutrients. These fertilizers contribute to soil health by enhancing microbial activity and promoting sustainable farming practices. However, their nutrient release is often slower compared to synthetic counterparts, requiring thoughtful planning to meet kale's specific growth demands.

Synthetic Fertilizers: Synthetic fertilizers offer precise control over nutrient concentrations and are readily available to plants. They provide a quick and targeted solution to nutrient deficiencies, which can be crucial for commercial kale production. However, over-reliance on synthetic fertilizers may lead to imbalances, soil degradation, and environmental concerns.

Many growers opt for a hybrid approach, combining organic and synthetic fertilizers to harness the benefits of both. This approach promotes sustainability while addressing immediate nutrient needs. Regardless of the chosen fertilizer type, proper application rates and timing are essential to prevent nutrient excesses or deficiencies.

Implementing Effective Fertilization Strategies

To optimize kale production for business, implementing effective fertilization strategies is paramount.

Precision Fertilization: Tailoring nutrient applications to the specific needs of the crop and growth stages is essential. Employing precision fertilization techniques, such as split applications or foliar feeding, ensures that kale receives nutrients when they are most beneficial. This approach maximizes nutrient use efficiency and minimizes waste.

Seasonal Adjustments: Recognizing the seasonal variations in nutrient requirements is crucial for successful kale cultivation. Adjusting fertilizer formulations and application rates based on seasonal demands, such as increased nitrogen during rapid growth periods, prevents nutrient imbalances and fosters healthy plant development.

Soil Amendments: Incorporating soil amendments, such as organic matter, helps improve soil structure and nutrient retention. This practice enhances the overall fertility of the soil, reducing the reliance on external fertilizers over time. Composted materials and cover crops are valuable additions that contribute to a sustainable and resilient nutrient management system.

Monitoring and Adaptation: Regular monitoring of soil nutrient levels, plant health, and growth patterns is fundamental for adapting fertilization strategies as needed. This proactive approach allows growers to identify potential issues before they escalate, ensuring a consistent and high-quality kale yield.

In conclusion, successful kale cultivation for business requires a comprehensive understanding of nutrient requirements, thoughtful selection of fertilizers, and the implementation of effective fertilization strategies. By combining knowledge of kale's growth stages with precision fertilization techniques, growers can optimize nutrient utilization, promote sustainable practices, and ultimately yield a bountiful harvest for the market.

CHAPTER NINE

HARVESTING TECHNIQUES ON Determining the Right Time to Harvest Kale

Introduction

Harvesting kale at the optimal time is crucial for ensuring peak freshness, flavor, and nutritional value. Determining the right time to harvest kale involves assessing various factors such as leaf size, color, and overall plant maturity.

Monitoring Leaf Size and Texture

One key indicator for harvesting kale is monitoring the size of the leaves. Kale leaves typically reach their peak size before they become tough or bitter. Harvesting leaves while they are still tender ensures a more pleasant eating experience. Pay attention to the texture as well; younger leaves tend to be softer and more palatable.

Observing Color Changes

The color of kale leaves can also provide valuable information about their readiness for harvest. While kale varieties may vary in color, a vibrant, deep green hue is often a sign of optimal maturity. Avoid harvesting leaves that appear yellowed or overly mature, as they may lack the desired tenderness and flavor.

Checking Overall Plant Maturity

Consider the overall maturity of the kale plant when determining the right time for harvest. Most varieties mature within 55 to 75 days after planting. Look for signs such as a well-developed central head or a bushy appearance for leafy varieties. Harvesting at this stage ensures that the plant has reached its full potential without risking over-maturation.

Harvesting Methods for Different Kale Varieties

Introduction

Kale comes in various varieties, each with unique characteristics. The harvesting methods for different kale varieties may vary based on their growth habits, leaf types, and intended use. Understanding these distinctions is crucial for optimizing yield and quality.

Curly Kale

Curly kale varieties, characterized by their tightly ruffled leaves, are a popular choice for salads and garnishes. When harvesting curly kale, focus on individual leaves rather than harvesting the entire plant. Use sharp scissors or pruning shears to snip leaves near the stem, allowing the plant to continue producing new growth.

Lacinato Kale

Lacinato kale, also known as dinosaur kale, has long, narrow, and slightly wrinkled leaves. Harvesting lacinato kale involves cutting the outer leaves first, starting from the bottom of the plant. This encourages upward growth and provides a continuous harvest over an extended period. Regular harvesting prevents the plant from becoming top-heavy and promotes a more robust structure.

Red Russian Kale

Red Russian kale is recognized for its purplish-red stems and fringed leaves. Harvesting this variety involves cutting the outer leaves while leaving the central leaves intact. This method ensures a balance between continuous harvest and maintaining the plant's vitality. Harvesting from the outside allows for better air circulation, reducing the risk of disease.

Post-Harvest Handling and Storage

Introduction

Post-harvest handling and storage play a crucial role in maintaining the quality and shelf life of harvested kale. Proper procedures can prevent wilting, decay, and nutrient loss, ensuring that the kale reaches consumers in optimal condition.

Cleaning and Washing

Upon harvest, it is essential to clean and wash kale thoroughly to remove dirt, debris, and any potential contaminants. Submerge the leaves in cold water, gently swishing them to dislodge impurities. Proper washing not only enhances the appearance of the kale but also contributes to its safety and longevity.

Drying and Removing Excess Moisture

After washing, it is important to dry the kale adequately. Excess moisture can lead to rot and decay during storage. Use a salad spinner or pat the leaves dry with clean towels. Ensure that the kale is completely dry before storing it in containers or packaging for distribution.

Proper Storage Conditions

Kale benefits from cold storage to maintain its crispness and nutritional value. Store kale in the refrigerator at temperatures around 32°F to 40°F (0°C to 4°C). Using perforated plastic bags or containers with ventilation holes helps regulate humidity and prevent condensation, preserving the kale's quality for an extended period.

Monitoring Shelf Life

Regularly monitor the shelf life of harvested kale to ensure that it is consumed or distributed before quality deterioration occurs. Check for signs of wilting, yellowing, or off odors, which may indicate spoilage. Proper post-harvest handling and storage practices contribute significantly to the marketability and consumer satisfaction of kale products.

CHAPTER TEN

MARKETING STRATEGIES FOR KALE PRODUCTS

Building a Brand for Your Kale Business

In the competitive landscape of the agricultural market, establishing a distinctive brand for your kale business is crucial for long-term success. A robust brand identity not only sets your products apart from competitors but also fosters customer loyalty. Begin by crafting a compelling brand story that reflects the essence of your kale products. Consider highlighting your commitment to sustainable farming practices, quality assurance, or any unique aspect of your cultivation process.

Invest in a memorable and visually appealing brand logo and packaging that communicates the freshness and nutritional value of your kale. Emphasize the health benefits and versatility of kale in various culinary applications. Utilize social media platforms to showcase behind-the-scenes glimpses of your kale farm, introducing the faces behind the business. Engage with your audience by sharing recipes, nutritional facts, and success stories related to your kale products.

Create a consistent brand voice across all communication channels, from your website and social media to packaging and marketing materials. Establishing a cohesive brand presence will contribute to brand recognition and make your kale products more memorable to consumers. Consider collaborating with influencers or nutritionists to endorse your brand and build credibility within the health and wellness community.

Targeting the Right Market Audience

Identifying and targeting the right market audience is a pivotal aspect of a successful kale business. Conduct thorough market research to understand the demographics, preferences, and purchasing behaviors of your potential customers. Kale appeals to health-conscious consumers, so focus on reaching individuals who prioritize a nutritious and balanced lifestyle. Tailor your marketing efforts to resonate with specific segments of the population, such as fitness enthusiasts, busy professionals, or parents seeking wholesome options for their families. Highlight the nutritional density of kale and its role in supporting overall well-being. Consider incorporating keywords related to health, organic farming, and sustainable practices in your marketing materials to attract environmentally conscious consumers.

Utilize data analytics and customer feedback to refine your target audience over time. Stay agile in adapting your marketing strategies to changing trends and consumer preferences. Leverage social media advertising to precisely target your audience based on factors such as age, location, and interests. By understanding and catering to the unique needs of your target market, you can build a more loyal customer base and drive sustainable growth for your kale business.

Developing Effective Marketing Campaigns

Crafting compelling marketing campaigns is essential to raise awareness and drive sales for your kale products. Start by creating a content calendar that aligns with key events, seasons, or health awareness months. For instance, develop campaigns around New Year's resolutions, summer wellness, or back-to-school nutrition.

Utilize a mix of online and offline marketing channels to maximize your reach. Leverage social media platforms to run visually appealing campaigns showcasing the versatility of kale in recipes, its nutritional benefits, and success stories from satisfied customers. Incorporate user-generated content by encouraging customers to share their kale-inspired creations with a branded hashtag.

Consider organizing events or workshops to educate your target audience about the health benefits of kale and provide hands-on experiences. Collaborate with local health and fitness influencers to host live cooking sessions or fitness challenges that feature your kale products. This not only enhances your brand visibility but also creates a sense of community around your kale business.

Implement promotions or discounts during strategic periods to incentivize trial purchases and foster customer loyalty. Leverage email marketing to keep your audience informed about new product launches, promotions, and relevant industry insights. By consistently delivering value through your marketing campaigns, you can position your kale business as a trusted and reputable choice in the market.

CHAPTER ELEVEN

FINANCIAL MANAGEMENT IN KALE FARMING

Budgeting and Cost Analysis in Kale Farming:

Budgeting is a critical aspect of financial management in kale farming. It involves estimating and allocating resources to various activities to ensure optimal production and profitability. In the context of kale farming, a well-structured budget helps farmers plan for expenses related to land preparation, seed acquisition, fertilizers, pesticides, labor, equipment, and other operational costs.

Cost analysis is integral to understanding the financial health of the kale farming venture. Farmers need to break down costs into fixed and variable components, enabling them to identify areas for cost reduction or optimization. This analysis aids in making informed decisions, such as negotiating better deals with suppliers or investing in technologies that improve efficiency.

Farmers should regularly review and update their budgets to reflect changes in market conditions, input costs, and other variables. This iterative process ensures that the budget remains a dynamic tool for financial management, helping kale farmers adapt to the ever-changing agricultural landscape.

Pricing Strategies for Kale Products:

Developing effective pricing strategies is essential for maximizing profits in the kale farming business. Several factors influence the pricing of kale products, including production costs, market demand, and competitors' prices.

Cost-Plus Pricing: One common strategy involves adding a markup to the production cost to determine the selling price. While straightforward, farmers must ensure that the markup is competitive in the market while covering all production expenses.

Market-Oriented Pricing: This strategy involves setting prices based on market conditions, demand,

and consumer preferences. Kale farmers need to stay informed about market trends and adjust their prices accordingly. This flexibility allows them to respond to changes in demand or shifts in consumer preferences.

Value-Based Pricing: This approach considers the perceived value of kale products by consumers. If the kale is grown using organic or sustainable practices, farmers may justify a higher price based on the perceived added value. Effective communication of these value-added aspects is crucial to implementing this strategy successfully.

Adopting a dynamic pricing strategy that considers both internal production costs and external market dynamics empowers kale farmers to find the right balance between competitiveness and profitability.

Financial Planning for Sustainable Growth in Kale

Farming:

Sustainable growth in kale farming requires careful financial planning to ensure the long-term viability of the business. This involves strategic allocation of resources, investment in technology and infrastructure, and diversification of revenue streams.

Investment in Technology: Incorporating technology into kale farming operations can improve efficiency and reduce long-term costs. Automated irrigation systems, precision farming techniques, and data analytics tools enable farmers to optimize resource use and enhance productivity.

Diversification of Revenue Streams: To mitigate risks associated with market fluctuations, kale farmers can explore diversifying their revenue streams. This could include selling value-added products like kale chips or establishing partnerships with local markets and restaurants to expand distribution channels.

Risk Management: Financial planning for sustainable growth necessitates a robust risk management strategy. Farmers should identify potential risks such as weather events, pest outbreaks, or market volatility and develop contingency plans to minimize the impact on their financial stability.

Financial Education and Consultation:

Constant learning and seeking professional financial advice are integral to successful financial planning. Farmers should stay updated on industry trends, attend workshops, and consult with financial experts to make informed decisions that align with their growth objectives.

In conclusion, successful financial management in kale farming involves meticulous budgeting, strategic pricing, and sustainable financial planning. By implementing these practices, kale farmers can navigate the complexities of the agricultural business and position themselves for long-term success.

CHAPTER TWELVE

SCALING UP AND DIVERSIFYING

Expanding Your Kale Farming Operation

Expanding your kale farming operation is a strategic move to meet the increasing demand for this nutrient-rich leafy green. As your business grows, you must carefully plan and execute the expansion process to ensure sustainability and profitability.

Market Analysis and Research

Before expanding, conduct a thorough market analysis to identify demand trends, consumer preferences, and potential competitors. Understanding the market dynamics will guide your expansion strategy, helping you choose the right scale and geographic location for your new operations.

Scaling Up Production

Consider increasing the acreage dedicated to kale cultivation. Evaluate your current production capacity and invest in additional resources such as land, machinery, and skilled labor. Implement efficient farming practices and leverage technology to streamline operations, ensuring a smooth transition to a larger scale.

Diversifying Varieties

Expanding your kale farm offers an opportunity to diversify your product portfolio. Introduce different kale varieties to cater to diverse consumer preferences. Experiment with heirloom varieties, and hybrid cultivars, or even consider organic options to tap into niche markets and differentiate your brand.

Establishing Partnerships

Forge partnerships with local distributors, grocery stores, or restaurants to secure a steady market for your expanded production. Building a network of reliable partners ensures a consistent revenue stream and strengthens your position in the supply chain.

Investing in Infrastructure

Upgrade your farm infrastructure to support increased production. This may include investing in irrigation systems, storage facilities, and transportation logistics. A well-equipped infrastructure ensures that your kale reaches the market in optimal condition, enhancing customer satisfaction and loyalty.

Diversifying Kale Products and Offerings

Diversifying kale products and offerings is a key strategy to enhance your business's competitiveness and appeal to a broader customer base. By exploring various product formats and value-added options, you can create new revenue streams and build a stronger brand presence.

Value-Added Kale Products

Explore the creation of value-added products like kale chips, kale smoothie blends, or pre-packaged salads. These products not only cater to consumers seeking convenience but also provide an avenue for premium pricing, boosting your overall profitability.

Launching Kale-Based Merchandise

Consider extending your brand beyond edible products. Develop merchandise such as branded kale recipe books, cooking utensils, or apparel. This not only generates additional income but also fosters brand loyalty and recognition among consumers.

Collaborations and Limited Editions

Collaborate with chefs, nutritionists, or influencers to create exclusive kale-based recipes or limited-edition products. This strategy can attract attention, generate buzz around your brand, and open up new market segments.

Expanding Distribution Channels

Diversify your distribution channels by exploring online platforms, farmers' markets, or specialty stores. This widens your reach and allows you to connect with different consumer demographics, further establishing your kale brand in the market.

Consumer Education Initiatives

Launch educational campaigns to inform consumers about the nutritional benefits of kale and creative ways to incorporate it into their diets. By fostering awareness, you not only drive demand for your existing products but also pave the way for future innovations.

Sustainable Practices for Long-Term Success

Embracing sustainable practices is not only a responsible choice for the environment but also a key factor in securing the long-term success of your kale farming business. Sustainable farming methods can improve efficiency, reduce costs, and enhance your brand reputation.

Implementing Organic Farming

Transitioning to organic farming practices can set your kale business apart in a market increasingly focused on sustainability. Organic kale is in high demand, and consumers are willing to pay a premium for produce grown without synthetic pesticides or fertilizers.

Water Conservation Strategies

Implement water-saving technologies such as drip irrigation and rainwater harvesting to reduce water usage on your farm. Efficient water management not only conserves a precious resource but also contributes to cost savings and environmental stewardship.

Zero-Waste Initiatives

Explore ways to minimize waste generation on your farm. This may involve composting crop residues, using waste for animal feed, or partnering with local businesses for waste recycling. Zero-waste initiatives not only benefit the environment but also demonstrate your commitment to responsible farming.

Sustainable Packaging Choices

Consider eco-friendly packaging options for your kale products. Biodegradable or recyclable packaging aligns with consumer preferences for sustainable choices and can enhance your brand image. Communicate your commitment to sustainability on packaging to appeal to environmentally conscious consumers.

Community Engagement and Social Responsibility

Engage with the local community through initiatives such as educational programs, farmer's markets, or collaborations with local schools. Demonstrating social responsibility enhances your brand's reputation, fosters community support, and contributes to the overall sustainability of your kale farming business.